THE THEORY OF LIFE

WHAT YOU'RE LIVING IS NOT LIFE

KOUSHIK AGARWALLA

Made with ♥ on the Notion Press Platform
www.notionpress.com

this book is dedicated to everyone who is still

searching for the purpose of their life.

Contents

Foreword

Within the pages of this profound book, Koushik invites you on a transformative journey of self-discovery. "The Theory Of Life" is a guiding light in a world often clouded by confusion, offering insights and practical tools to help you unlock your true potential. With compassion and wisdom, Koushik explores life's purpose and provides a roadmap for finding meaning, joy, and fulfillment. Prepare to embark on a remarkable adventure that will forever change the way you perceive yourself and the world around you. Through personal anecdotes, thought-provoking reflections, and timeless wisdom, Koushik delves into the depths of our existence, unraveling the mysteries of life with clarity and profound insight. With every turn of the page, you will gain a deeper understanding of yourself, uncover the interconnectedness of all things, and embrace the transformative power that lies within you. "The Theory Of Life" is not just a book, it is a catalyst for personal growth, a companion on your journey towards self-realization, and a testament to the boundless potential that awaits you. Get ready to embark on an extraordinary voyage of self-discovery and awaken to the limitless possibilities that life has to offer. In this beautifully crafted book, Koushik skillfully weaves together modern wisdom and contemporary insights, offering a timeless roadmap for navigating the complexities of life. With heartfelt guidance and practical exercises, you will be empowered to break free from limiting beliefs, embrace your unique powers, and create a life that aligns with your deepest aspirations. "The Theory Of Life" is an invitation to embark on a soul-stirring quest, where you will not only discover your life's purpose but also learn to live it with passion, authenticity, and unwavering clarity. Prepare to embark on a remarkable journey of self-discovery and transformation, where the pages of this book will become a compass, guiding you towards a life of meaning, joy, and profound fulfillment.

Preface

When contemplating the profound mysteries of existence, we often find ourselves immersed in a sea of questions. What is the purpose of life? Why are we here? What does it mean to truly live? These timeless inquiries have captivated humanity for centuries, sparking a quest for understanding and meaning. "The Theory of Life" is born out of a deep desire to explore these profound questions and to offer a fresh perspective on the intricacies of our existence. As the author of this book, I have delved into the realms of philosophy, science, spirituality, and personal experience to craft a comprehensive framework that aims to shed light on the tapestry of life. While "The Theory of Life" does not purport to provide all the answers, it offers a guiding hand, a compass, to navigate the depths of existence. It invites you to engage in a dynamic dialogue with the concepts presented, encouraging you to embark on your own introspective journey and find resonance with the insights shared. The driving force behind this book is not to assert a singular truth but to ignite the flame of inquiry within each reader. It is an invitation to embark on a personal quest for meaning and purpose, encouraging you to explore your own unique experiences, beliefs, and perceptions.

I invite you to approach this book with an open mind and a sense of wonder. As we embark on this intellectual and spiritual expedition together, may we uncover profound insights, challenge our assumptions, and, ultimately, discover a deeper connection to ourselves, to one another, and to the grand tapestry of existence.

Acknowledgements

I would like to express my deepest gratitude to the individuals who have played a pivotal role in the creation of this book, "The Theory of Life." Their unwavering support, encouragement, and love have been instrumental in bringing this project to fruition.

First and foremost, I would like to thank my parents for their belief in me and their unwavering support throughout this journey.

To my uncle, Tarun Agarwal, your advices, mentorship, and thought-provoking ideas have profoundly influenced my intellectual growth.

I would also like to extend my heartfelt appreciation to Priency Di and Riri. Your unwavering encouragement and belief in my abilities have been invaluable. Your insightful conversations and willingness to share your own experiences have enriched my understanding and provided me with the inspiration to explore new realms of thought. Thank you for standing by me through the highs and lows of this creative endeavor.

Not to forget, Jeeban and Sachi, whom I deeply miss. Over the span of five years, you both have been instrumental in my life, offering constant support, guidance, and friendship. I cherish the memories we've shared, from our late-night discussions to the joyous moments of laughter. I can't help but wish that we could have more time together. Additionally, I extend my heartfelt thanks to Mota Bhai (Vinit) for his presence and encouragement in my life. Your contributions have made my journey as a writer and as a person more meaningful. To all of you, thank you for being such an integral part of my life. I treasure our friendship beyond words.

To all the teachers, mentors, and friends who have contributed to my intellectual and personal growth, I extend my deepest gratitude. Your guidance, knowledge, and support have shaped my journey and have played a significant role in shaping the ideas presented in this book.

Lastly, I would like to express my appreciation to the readers. Your curiosity, open-mindedness, and willingness to explore the depths of life's mysteries are the fuel that drives my passion for sharing knowledge and insights. It is my sincerest hope that "The Theory of Life" resonates with you, provokes thoughtful contemplation, and offers a fresh perspective on the profound questions that permeate our existence.

Without the support and contributions of each and every one of you, this book would not have been possible. Thank you for believing in me, inspiring me, and being an integral part of this transformative journey.

Yours truly,
Koushik

Prologue

Have you ever found yourself pondering the profound mysteries of existence? The purpose of life, the intricacies of consciousness, the interconnectedness of all things? If so, then welcome to a captivating journey—the pages of "The Theory of Life" are here to ignite your curiosity and unveil a fresh perspective on the enigmatic tapestry of our existence.

"The Theory of Life" does not claim to hold all the answers, for life's mysteries are as vast and awe-inspiring as the cosmos itself. Instead, it offers a captivating lens through which we can explore, ponder, and marvel at the grand tapestry of existence. It beckons you, dear reader, to embrace the unknown, to embark on a transformative journey of self-discovery, and to uncover profound insights that will forever reshape your perception of reality.

Welcome to the boundless adventure that awaits within "The Theory of Life."

the purpose of life

I always believed that the only purpose of life is to be happy.

Isn't it? Why else go through all the pain and difficulties? It's only to achieve happiness in some or the other way.

And I'm not the only one who believed that. Genuinely speaking, if you look around you, majority of the people are pursuing happiness in their lives.

That's why we collectively buy shit we don't actually need, watch movies with no logical context, and try to work hard to get approval and acceptability of people we don't really like to be or work with.

Have you ever thought of it that why do we do these things? To be honest, I don't give a damn what the exact reason is. I'm neither a scientist nor a doc. All I know is that it has something to do with history, environment, science, media, economy, psychology, politics, the information era, and you name it. The list is never ending.

Accept Yourself.

Let's just live with the fact. Most people love to figure out why people are not happy or don't live fulfilling lives. I don't care about the why.

I care more about *how* we can change.

Just a year ago, I tried everything to chase happiness.

- You get a package from Amazon, and you think that makes you happy.
- You get a high-paying job you don't really are interested in, and think that makes you happy.
- You go on holiday for a week, and you think that makes you happy.
- You go to Pizza Hut or McDonald's, and you think that makes you happy

But at the end of the day, you're on your bed (trying to sleep), and you think: "What's next in this endless mission of chasing happiness?"

Well, let me help you with your question: You, chasing something random that you believe makes you happy.

It's all illusion. A bluff. A lie that's been just made up to fool people.

Did **Hugo Black** (most probably you don't know him) lie to us when he said:

> *"The very first condition of lasting happiness is that a life should be full of purpose, aiming at something outside self."*

I think we should look at this quote from a different angle. Because when you read it, you think that happiness is the main goal. And that's kind of what the quote says as well.

But here's the catch: How do you attain happiness?

Happiness can't be a target or goal in itself. Thus, it's not something that's achievable.

I believe that happiness is merely a consequence of usefulness.

When I talk about this theory with friends, family, and teachers, I always find it tough to put my thoughts into words. But I'll give it a shot here.

Most of the things we do in life are just tasks and experiences.

- You go on a trip.
- You go to office or college.
- You go for dinner.
- You go shopping.
- You buy a new car.
- You get the latest iPhone or Mac for no reason.
- You go clubbing.

Those things do make you elated, right? But they are not at all useful. You're not creating or producing anything. You're just consuming or doing something. And that's great.

Don't get me wrong. I love to go on trips too, or get a new pair of Jordans. But to be frank, it's not what gives meaning to my life.

What really makes me happy is when I'm useful and productive. When I produce something that others can utilise (just like this article). Or even when I create something I can utilise to become a better version of myself.

I found it very difficult to explain the concept of happiness in life. But when I recently ran into a quote by Leo Rosten, the thoughts finally connected.

> *""The purpose of life is not to be happy—but to matter, to be productive, to be useful, to have it make some difference that you lived at all.""*

And I didn't understand this before I became more aware of what I'm doing with my life. And that always sounds heavy and shit. But it's actually really plain and simple.

It draws down to this: What are you DOING that's making a difference to others or yourself ?

Have you ever done any useful thing in your lifetime? You don't have to change the world or anything. Just make it a little bit better than before you came in this world.

If you don't know how, here are some tips.

- Help someone near you with something that's not your responsibility.
- Create an album of pictures (not a digital one) .
- Workout on yourself everyday(both, physically and mentally)
- Write down on a paper about the stuff you learned in life.
- Call your friend or family and ask if you can help with something.
- Build something yourself at home instead of purchasing it.
- Start teaching poor children and treat them well.

That's just some stuff I can think of . You can create a list of your own useful activities.

You see? It's not anything extraordinary. But when you do little useful things every day, it sums up to a life that is well lived. A life that matters and has a meaning.

Recently I went through an extract of the book *Not Fade Away* by Laurence Shames. It's about Peter Barton, the founder of Liberty Media, who shares his thoughts about dying from cancer.

It's a very impactful book and it will definitely bring you to the edge. In the book, he talks about how he lived his life and how he found his calling. He went to a business school, and this is what he thought of his fellow MBA candidates:

"Bottom line: they were extremely bright people who would never really do anything, would never add much to society, would leave no legacy behind. I found this terribly sad, in the way that wasted potential is always sad."

You can state that for almost all of us. And after realising this in his thirties, he started a company that turned him into a multi-billionaire.

Another personality who always proves himself useful is **Casey Neistat**. For near three years he posted new videos regularly about his life and work on YouTube. And in every video, he's doing something.

He also mentions about how he always wants to do something productive. He even has a tattoo on his arm that says *"Do More."*

On the other hand most people would say, "Why would you work more?" And then they turn on Netflix or Amazon Prime and binge-watch episodes of the latest series or an Anime (for an Otaku) that came out.

The Ideal mindset.

Being useful or productive is a mindset. And like with any mindset, it starts with a decision and also some challenges. One day I woke up and thought to myself: What am I doing for this world? The answer was nothing.

And the very same day I started writing. For you it can be speaking, painting, inventing something, helping someone, or anything you feel like doing.

Don't take it too seriously. It's nothing to overthink. Just DO something that's useful. ANYTHING.

what are you running away from?

What are we running away from? Everyone will have their own answers to this question like People, Problems, Work, and Difficulties etc.

But it's none of these. We are running away from **SUCCESS**. You might think that I am wrong but give it a thought. These problems or difficulties you are going through are just intermediaries between you and success. Isn't it?

So, suppose you are in block zero and then you start working towards something (might be money, or a competitive exam or an award etc), you will face an endless list of difficulties and problems which will scare you and make you doubt your ability. And, this is when most of the people tend to turn back and stop working which again moves you back to block zero.

Then, there are certain people who face those difficulties, without getting scared and take careful steps to cross these problems and boom. They are standing at the gate of their goal all open just for them.

If you run away from the problems, you are only going to hit the wall on the opposite side, and fall straight on the ground. This wall is called "**WALL OF YOUR INNER FEARS**".

On the other hand:

If you go and hug the problems and face it, the problems can show you any or all of the 3 things told below:

1. **Opportunities** - The heap of opportunities lying behind the problem.
2. **Life lessons** - Can teach you any life lessons if you have missed.
3. **Builds Strength & Character** - Makes you strong enough to fight and face for anything in future.

These obstacles are just like **Black holes**, you cannot run away from it. Can you? (or maybe ask yourself, *Should you run away from it?*)

The more you will run, the bigger it will become.

In the end, it will become so huge that you will finally have to face it and probably you will fail miserably.

Consider this scenario:-

In a 100m sprintdash **(Round 1)** there are 10 athletes contesting and you are one among them.

The remaining 9 athletes are posing a problem to you. Once you try to run away from them and secure the podium, you get promoted to **Round 2.** Now new problems arise!

Problems keep coming until you win the final race. After winning you won't get relived as you have another league to prepare for. **This continues forever!**

But the actual athletes don't see them as a problem. They consider it as their **profession and passion** (to solve the problem) because that (problem) is what which takes them to the next level.

If you become passionate and consistent towards solving your problems you will definitely reach the next level of achievement and success.

<u>The best way To Become RICH</u>

According to Marwari (*it's a caste practiced in India*) logic,

- If you sell a single cup of tea:

Production cost = ? 3, Selling cost= ? 10, Profit= ? 7

- If 500 cups of tea are sold in a day:

Profit in a day = Three thousands and five hundred rupees.

Profit in a month = One lakh and five thousand rupees.

Profit in a year = **Twelve lakh and sixty thousand INR.**

So, it's time to roll that degree and say,

"Chai chai, garam chai."

NOTE: This case was just for fun and not in a serious note.

If you are still here, I will assume that you are interested to dig deeper. Isn't it? (*I bet you won't regret investing your time reading ahead*)

So, you want to finally discover how to be successful?

First, imagine where you will honestly be in next five years.

Maybe on a beach, working remotely while having fresh coconut water on your other hand. Or maybe you will be sitting on a couch, binge-watching Netflix, and still dreaming.

WHAT IS SUCCESS?

Everyone has their own definition for success. Maybe for you, you want to succeed financially and some may want it socially or philosophically. (*Again, there's an endless list for meanings of success*)

Being successful isn't necessarily about being rich or winning National Awards. It can be also about personal satisfaction or fulfilment.

For example, if you had to design your perfect day, what would it look like?

Would you be sitting on a bench next to some lake reading Colleen Hoover? Do you imagine yourself trekking and taking that big, deep breath once you reach to the end? Or maybe you just want to spend your entire day next to your family?

As I mentioned earlier, everyone has their own definitions for success and the other people's definition are not meant for your success, Right?

Whatever it is, that'll make you feel happy and fulfilled is what you need to focus on while on the way to attaining success.

IMPORTANCE OF SUCCESS?

Most people just obsess over how to be successful because we all want to feel like we matter. Without achieving any success, we might look back at our life, disappointed on ourselves for not making an impact.

The goal of achieving success will help you live a more purposeful life by pushing you to face and overcome all the obstacles, work harder and pursue happiness.

<u>What does it take to be Successful ?</u>

Nothing will motivate you more than a feeling of rage and jealousy inside you. (*to prove your criticisers wrong, let's go*)

So here's your diss: You spend way too much time on unimportant things while pretending that you're 'researching or learning/finding motivation.' But the truth is, you're slacking. And you're never going to get your shit together unless you START WORKING TOWARDS YOUR GOAL. So, if you want to travel the world, have 2-3 supercars(*McLaren Elva, Ferrari Monza etc*), a sneaker-wall (full of *Jordans* and *Yeezys)*, it's never going to happen if you don't take that first step you are avoiding or the problems you are running away from.

That's it.

what if you fail?

Ready to dive into a topic that's often swept under the rug ? **the magnificent world of failure**. I know what you're thinking: "Why would I want to read about failure?" But hang on a second readers, because failure isn't the enemy—it's actually the key to unlocking your true potential.

Imagine standing at the edge of the unknown, heart pounding with excitement and dreams of success racing through your mind. With a surge of courage, you take that daring leap towards your goals. It's an adrenaline rush—the thrill of chasing your dreams and conquering any obstacles in your path.

But here's the thing we rarely talk about—what if you stumble and fall, despite giving it your all? We've been taught to fear failure, like it's some kind of life-ruining monster. But guess what? It's time to flip the script and embrace failure like a boss.

Let me give you the lowdown. Throughout history, incredible people who've left their mark on the world have faced failure head-on. Take a guy named **Thomas Edison**, the genius behind the light bulb. He once said,

"I have not failed. I've just found 10,000 ways that won't work."

Can you imagine if he'd let failure get him down? We'd still be fumbling around in the dark!

So, here's the deal—failure isn't the end of the road. It's actually a stepping stone on the path to greatness. Failure gives us valuable lessons, teaches us resilience, and helps us grow stronger than ever before.

Now, I won't sugarcoat it—failure can suck big time. It bruises our pride and makes us doubt ourselves. But guess what? It's in those moments when we feel like we're at rock bottom that we discover our true strength. Failure is like a wake-up call, telling us to rise up, shake off the dust, and unleash our hidden potential.

Here's the secret sauce: *perseverance.* You've got to keep going, keep pushing, even when things seem impossible. Embrace failure as a necessary part of the journey, not as a sign of defeat. It's the rocky road that leads to greatness—the rough draft before the masterpiece.

But hey, let's get one thing straight: failure doesn't define you. It's just a chapter in your story, not the whole book. Failure is like a detour that takes you on unexpected adventures, introduces new characters, and helps you become the person you were always meant to be.

So, whether you're a dreamer in your teens or a young-at-heart adventurer, remember this: failure is not the end—it's the beginning of something extraordinary. It's a chance to learn, to grow, and to kick some serious butt. Keep hustling, keep dreaming, and embrace the beautiful messiness of life. Failure is just a part of the epic journey we're all on.

So, buckle up, folks, because failure is about to become your secret weapon on the road to epic success.

is money everything ?

In the vibrant tapestry of Indian life, there exists a question that jumps within us all: **Is money everything?** In a world where financial success often takes center stage, it's easy to get caught up in the pursuit of wealth. But deep down, we know that there is more to life than the mere accumulation of material riches. So, let us embark on an enlightening journey together as we explore real-life situations that will challenge our preconceived notions and reveal the true essence of wealth.

<u>*A TALE OF TWO LIVES*</u>

In the heart of bustling Indian cities, let us meet Rajesh, a young and ambitious entrepreneur who has achieved remarkable financial success. With a burgeoning bank balance and a lifestyle that exudes luxury, Rajesh seems to have it all. Yet, beneath the surface, there is a lingering sense of emptiness. Despite his material abundance, Rajesh longs for something deeper—an intangible sense of purpose and fulfillment that money alone cannot provide. It is in this quest for significance that he begins to realize that true wealth lies not in the digits on a balance sheet, but in the experiences money cannot buy—the joy of helping others, the satisfaction of making a positive impact on the world, and the connections forged with loved ones.

Now, let us turn our attention to Deepa, a humble teacher in a small village school. While her salary may not be substantial, her impact is immeasurable. Deepa finds true wealth in the smiles of her students, in the knowledge she imparts, and in the transformation she inspires. It is in the classroom, amidst the eager minds of her young charges, that she discovers a wealth beyond monetary measures. Deepa reminds us that true wealth is not solely tied to financial prosperity, but rather to the imprint we leave on the lives of others and the difference we make in our communities.

FINDING WEALTH IN RELATIONS

In the colorful mosaic of Indian culture, we find that wealth is often intricately woven into the tapestry of relationships. Let us venture into the lives of Nisha and Amit, an ordinary middle-class couple residing in a bustling metropolis. Though they may not possess the material luxuries that wealth can bring, their lives are enriched by a different kind of abundance—a wealth defined by the strength of their bond, the shared joys and sorrows, and the unwavering support they offer one another. It is in the simple moments of togetherness, the laughter shared over a cup of *chai*, and the love that enters their daily lives that Nisha and Amit discover a wealth that transcends the confines of monetary measures. Their story reminds us that true wealth resides in the depth of our relationships and the connections we nurture with our loved ones.

THE JOURNEY OF SELF DISCOVERY

Beyond the pursuit of material gain, many of us embark on a personal journey of self-discovery—a quest to uncover what true wealth means to us. Let us now follow the path of Reena, a young artist with dreams that stretch beyond societal expectations. Despite facing financial challenges, Reena's passion for her craft remains unwavering. In the midst of adversity, she discovers a wealth that money cannot diminish—the freedom to express herself creatively, the joy of bringing her artistic visions to life, and the fulfillment that comes from pursuing her true calling. Reena's journey teaches us that true wealth lies not in the accumulation of monetary riches, but in the pursuit of our passions and the alignment of our lives with our innermost desires.

MAKING A DIFFERENECE

Within the diverse curtains of Indian society, we often find that true wealth manifests in the impact we have on the lives of others. Let us now shine a light on Ravi, a compassionate social worker committed to uplifting the underprivileged. Ravi's wealth is not measured by the digits in his bank account, but rather by the lives he touches, the smiles he brings, and the positive change he fosters in the world around him. Through his tireless efforts, Ravi discovers that true wealth lies in making a difference—whether it be providing education to those in need, offering a helping hand to the marginalized, or inspiring hope in the hearts of the disheartened. His story serves as a testament that true wealth is found in the meaningful contributions we make to society and the lasting impact we leave behind.

Thus, as we journey through the lives of Rajesh, Deepa, Nisha and Amit, Reena, and Ravi, a profound truth emerges—the true essence of wealth extends far beyond the mere accumulation of money. It lies in the experiences that money cannot buy, the relationships we nurture, the pursuit of our passions, and the impact we have on the lives of others. True wealth encompasses a tapestry of connections, purpose, and contribution.

So, let us resist the temptation to equate wealth solely with monetary measures. Instead, let us seek a harmonious balance—one that acknowledges the importance of financial stability while embracing the richness that lies beyond material riches. By cultivating meaningful relationships, pursuing our passions, and making a positive impact, we unlock the true wealth that resides within us and create a life of genuine prosperity and fulfillment.

the art of letting go the fears

Life is a journey filled with ups and downs, victories, and challenges. As humans, we all face fears and insecurities that hold us back from truly experiencing life. In this book, we explore the art of letting go - the ability to release our fears and embrace life wholeheartedly. Through relatable stories and thought-provoking exercises, we aim to guide Indian readers on a transformative path, empowering them to confront their fears, make choices that resonate with their true selves, and create a life filled with happiness and satisfaction.

RECOGNIZNG THE FEARS THAT HOLD YOU BACK

We all have fears that hold us back from pursuing our dreams and living life to the fullest. Picture this: You have always dreamt of starting your own business, but the fear of failure and financial insecurity constantly lingers in your mind. It stops you from taking that leap of faith and pursuing your passion. Can you relate?

Take a moment to reflect on your own life and think about the fears that have prevented you from stepping outside your comfort zone. Perhaps you've been afraid to express your true feelings to someone you care about, fearing rejection or heartbreak. These fears can be deeply ingrained, and it takes courage to confront them.

Now, let's dig deeper. Imagine a time when fear held you back from an incredible opportunity. Maybe you had a chance to travel to a new country, but the fear of the unknown and leaving your familiar surroundings made you hesitate. Reflect on how that fear impacted your decision-making and the experiences you missed out on.

It's important to recognize that fears can come from various sources—past experiences, societal expectations, or self-doubt. Maybe you've been conditioned to believe that certain career paths are more secure and prestigious, causing you to fear pursuing your true passion. Identifying these fears allows you to understand their roots and work towards overcoming them.

Consider the emotions tied to your fears. Fear often masks deeper emotions like insecurity or the fear of failure. Think about how these emotions have affected your choices and actions in various areas of your life, whether it's relationships, career, or personal growth. By acknowledging these emotions, you can better understand the impact they have on your decision-making process.

Remember, you're not alone in experiencing these fears. Many individuals have faced similar obstacles and managed to overcome them. By recognizing your fears and understanding their influence on your life, you can take the first step towards letting go and embracing a life free from unnecessary limitations.

QUESTIONING LIMITING BELIEFS

We often hold onto limiting beliefs that restrict our potential and keep us trapped in fear. Think about a belief you have that limits your abilities or holds you back from pursuing your goals. It could be the belief that you're not smart enough, talented enough, or deserving of success. Sound familiar?

Now, let's challenge these beliefs together. Take a moment to consider the evidence supporting these limiting beliefs. Are they based on facts or just perceptions? Often, we create these beliefs based on past experiences or the opinions of others, without realizing that they don't define our true capabilities.

Reflect on how these limiting beliefs have influenced your choices and actions. Have they caused you to play it safe, avoid taking risks, or settle for less than what you truly desire? It's time to question the validity of these beliefs and understand that you have the power to redefine them.

Consider the source of these limiting beliefs. Have you absorbed them from family, friends, or societal expectations? We often internalize these beliefs without realizing their negative impact on our lives. By identifying the origins of these beliefs, you can detach yourself from their influence and start reshaping your own beliefs based on your true potential.

Now, let's explore alternative perspectives and counterexamples. Seek evidence of individuals who have overcome similar challenges or achieved success despite circumstances aligned with your limiting beliefs. By exposing yourself to inspiring stories and examples, you expand your mindset and open yourself up to new possibilities.

Remember, you have the power to challenge and replace limiting beliefs with empowering ones. By questioning these beliefs, you create room for personal growth, self-discovery, and the realization of your true potential.

EMBRACING VULNERABILITY AS STRENGTH

We all experience the fear of vulnerability—the fear of being seen, of opening ourselves up emotionally, and risking rejection or judgment. Think back to a time when you were afraid to show your true self. Maybe it was in a new friendship or a romantic relationship. Can you recall the vulnerability that made you hesitant?

Consider the underlying emotions tied to your fear of vulnerability. Was it the fear of rejection, the fear of getting hurt, or the fear of not being accepted for who you truly are? These emotions are relatable, as many of us have experienced them at some point in our lives.

Now, imagine what could have happened if you had embraced vulnerability instead of hiding behind a facade. Reflect on the missed opportunities for connection, growth, and deep relationships that may have resulted from your fear. Embracing vulnerability allows you to experience authentic connections and genuine experiences that enrich your life.

It's important to challenge the notion that vulnerability is a weakness. Instead, view it as a strength—a testament to your courage, authenticity, and emotional intelligence. Embracing vulnerability requires a shift in mindset, where you recognize that your true worth lies not in protecting yourself, but in embracing your genuine self.

Consider role models or personalities who have embraced vulnerability and experienced personal growth as a result. Think about their stories and how their openness has led to meaningful connections and opportunities. These stories serve as reminders that vulnerability can lead to profound personal growth, deeper connections, and a more fulfilling life.

By reframing vulnerability as a source of strength, you can gradually break down the barriers that fear has built and create space for authenticity, growth, and meaningful connections with yourself and others. Remember, vulnerability is a shared human experience, and embracing it can lead to incredible personal and emotional growth.

DEVELOPING A POSITIVE MINDSET FOR GROWTH

Having a positive mindset is crucial in the journey of letting go of fear and embracing a fulfilling life. Imagine a recent setback or failure you experienced. Maybe you didn't get the promotion you were hoping for, or a project didn't go as planned. Reflect on how you initially reacted to that situation. Did you view it as a learning opportunity or as a reflection of your worth?

Now, let's shift our perspective. Instead of seeing setbacks as reasons to retreat into fear, view them as opportunities for growth. Consider how the setback could have provided valuable lessons and insights. By embracing a positive mindset, you can transform setbacks into stepping stones toward success.

Think about individuals who have faced adversity and come out stronger on the other side. Reflect on their stories and the resilience they demonstrated. Their experiences show us that a positive mindset can help us overcome challenges and move forward with determination.

Cultivating a growth mindset involves challenging negative self-talk and limiting beliefs. Consider the internal dialogue that occurs when you face a new challenge or opportunity. Are you quick to doubt yourself or dwell on potential failure? Recognize these negative thought patterns and consciously replace them with more positive and empowering thoughts.

Another aspect of cultivating a growth mindset is embracing the concept of "yet." When faced with a new skill or opportunity, avoid saying, "I can't do it." Instead, add the word "yet" to the end of the sentence. For example, "I can't do it yet." This simple shift in language acknowledges that growth and learning are ongoing processes.

Remember, a positive mindset is not about denying the existence of challenges or setbacks; it's about approaching them with resilience, optimism, and a belief in your ability to overcome them. By cultivating a positive mindset, you create a foundation for personal growth, resilience, and a life lived without the shackles of fear.

TAKE ACTIONS

Letting go of fear and embracing a fulfilling life requires taking action and stepping outside your comfort zone. Consider a dream or goal that has been lingering in your heart, but fear has prevented you from pursuing it. Maybe it's starting a new business, traveling to a foreign country, or pursuing a creative passion. Can you relate to the hesitation and fear that arise when considering such endeavors?

Now, it's time to break free from the grip of fear and take small, actionable steps towards your aspirations. Think about the first step you can take today to move closer to your dream. It could be researching, making a phone call, or creating a plan. Taking that initial step, no matter how small, creates momentum and builds confidence.

Consider the stories of individuals who have taken bold leaps and stepped into the unknown. Reflect on how their courage and willingness to take risks led to transformative experiences and personal growth. Their stories serve as inspiration and reminders that great things can happen when we embrace uncertainty.

Recognize that growth and progress often happen outside of your comfort zone. Stepping into the unknown can be intimidating, but it also presents opportunities for self-discovery and new experiences. Embrace the discomfort and trust in your ability to adapt and navigate through unfamiliar territory.

Remember, taking action doesn't guarantee immediate success or the absence of challenges. However, every step forward is an opportunity for learning, growth, and self-empowerment. Celebrate your progress along the way and acknowledge the courage it takes to move beyond fear.

By taking consistent action and stepping into the unknown, you gradually expand your comfort zone and open yourself up to a world of possibilities. Letting go of fear becomes a transformative journey, where you create a life filled with purpose, fulfillment, and the freedom to embrace new adventures.

In conclusion, by recognizing our fears, cultivating a positive mindset, embracing vulnerability, and taking action, we can let go of the fears that hold us back and embark on a remarkable journey of self-discovery and growth. These chapters are designed to be relatable, drawing from common experiences and real-life situations that readers like you can relate to. Remember, the power to let go and create a fulfilling life lies within you.

• 25 •

the beauty of simplicity

Life can get overwhelming with countless responsibilities, expectations, and distractions. Amidst this chaos, we often overlook the beauty and tranquility that comes from embracing simplicity. In this chapter, we will explore the power of simplicity and how it can bring happiness and fulfillment to our lives. Through relatable stories and vivid situations that resonate with Indian readers, we will discover the extraordinary moments hidden within the simplicity of everyday life.

CLEARING OUT THE CLUTTER

Imagine your home cluttered with clothes you no longer wear, gadgets collecting dust, and books piled high. This clutter not only takes up physical space but also creates mental and emotional clutter. Now, picture yourself decluttering and simplifying your surroundings. Feel the sense of liberation as you let go of unnecessary possessions, creating room for what truly brings you joy. Visualize the unburdened space and the peace that accompanies it.

Remember the wise words of Mahatma Gandhi:

""The more you have, the more you are occupied;
the less you have, the more free you are.""

Reflect on the freedom and contentment that come from living with less. Envision a life where you value experiences over material possessions, finding true happiness in the simplicity of your surroundings.

EMBRACING A SIMPLE LIFESTYLE

Close your eyes and imagine starting your day with a peaceful morning ritual. Picture yourself practicing meditation or yoga, feeling the calmness wash over you. Now, visualize enjoying a simple, nourishing breakfast, savoring each bite mindfully. Feel the sense of serenity and clarity that accompanies this intentional start to your day.

Think about how embracing simplicity in your daily routine can alleviate stress and enhance your well-being. Picture yourself slowing down, prioritizing what truly matters, and approaching each task with a renewed sense of focus. Imagine the profound impact that simplicity can have on your overall sense of peace and happiness.

Drawing inspiration from the teachings of Swami Vivekananda, embrace simplicity as the secret to success. Imagine a life where you make space for what truly matters, freeing yourself from the constant pursuit of busyness. Visualize a simpler lifestyle that allows you to cherish the present moment and find contentment in the ordinary.

FINIDNG JOY IN SIMPLE PLEASURES

Take a moment to recall the simple pleasures that bring a smile to your face. Visualize the warmth of a cup of tea on a rainy day, the laughter of loved ones filling the air, or the breathtaking beauty of a vibrant sunset. Imagine fully immersing yourself in these moments, savoring the extraordinary magic hidden within life's simplest joys.

Often, we chase after grand adventures and extraordinary experiences, seeking happiness in the extraordinary. But true happiness lies in appreciating the ordinary and finding joy in the little things. Visualize a life where you pause to notice the beauty around you—the delicate blooming of a flower, the gentle touch of a loved one, or the sound of raindrops on your windowpane. See how these simple moments fill your heart with gratitude and happiness.

Embrace the wisdom of Rabindranath Tagore:

> *"Clouds come floating into my life, no longer to carry rain or usher storm, but to add color to my sunset sky."*

Imagine a life where you embrace simplicity, finding extraordinary moments in the ordinary. Let these moments of simplicity illuminate your path, bringing you lasting joy, fulfillment, and a profound appreciation for the beauty that surrounds you every day.

make it happen

Life is a canvas waiting to be painted with the strokes of our dreams and aspirations. In the journey of turning our aspirations into reality, we often find ourselves faced with doubts, fears, and a lack of motivation. But deep within each one of us lies the power to make things happen, to shape our own destinies. In this book, we will embark on a transformative exploration of how to ignite that power within ourselves. Through relatable stories, thought-provoking situations, and interactive reflections, we will uncover the tools and mindset needed to take action, overcome obstacles, and create the life we truly desire.

THE POWER OF INTENTION

Setting clear intentions is the first step towards making things happen and creating the life we desire. It is about aligning our thoughts, emotions, and actions with our deepest aspirations. Through relatable stories, thought-provoking situations, and interactive reflections, we will explore the profound impact that intention can have on our lives.

Imagine waking up each morning with a sense of purpose and direction. Setting intentions provides us with a clear roadmap, guiding our actions and decisions throughout the day. It allows us to focus our energy and attention on what truly matters to us. Reflect on a time when you set a powerful intention and experienced the positive effects it had on your actions and outcomes.

For instance, consider someone who set the intention to cultivate more gratitude in their life. They made a conscious effort to appreciate the little things, express gratitude to others, and keep a gratitude journal. As a result, they noticed a significant shift in their overall perspective, feeling more content and joyful.

Between the paragraphs, take a moment to reflect on the intentions you've set for your own life. Are they aligned with your deepest desires and values? Are there any intentions that need to be reevaluated or refined? Reflect on how setting clear intentions can serve as a compass, guiding your actions and decisions towards the life you desire.

Visualization is a powerful tool that can enhance the effectiveness of our intentions. By vividly imagining our desired outcomes, we create a mental blueprint that helps manifest our goals. Close your eyes and imagine yourself in a situation where you have achieved a significant goal or fulfilled a cherished dream. Visualize the details—the sights, sounds, and emotions associated with that experience.

For example, if your intention is to travel to a specific destination, visualize yourself stepping off the plane, feeling the warmth of the sun on your skin, and immersing yourself in the local culture. By repeatedly visualizing these images, you strengthen your belief in the possibility of your intention coming to fruition.

Setting intentions requires us to confront and overcome our limiting beliefs. These beliefs often stem from past experiences, societal conditioning, or self-doubt. They create a mental barrier that holds us back from fully embracing our desires and taking action.

Think about a specific goal or dream you have. What limiting beliefs are holding you back from pursuing it? Is it a fear of failure, a sense of unworthiness, or the belief that it's too late to start? Identify these beliefs and challenge their validity. Remind yourself that you are capable of achieving your intentions, regardless of any perceived limitations.

While reading, reflect on the limiting beliefs that are currently impeding your progress. Write them down and then reframe them as positive affirmations. For example, if your belief is "I'm not good enough," reframe it as "I am worthy of pursuing my dreams, and I have the skills and resources to make them happen." Repeat these affirmations daily to shift your mindset and align it with your intentions.

Intentions without action remain mere wishes. To manifest our intentions, we must take aligned action towards our desired outcomes. Reflect on the steps you can take today to bring your intentions to life. Break them down into smaller, manageable tasks that move you closer to your goals.

Consider the story of an individual who set the intention to improve their physical fitness. They committed to a regular exercise routine, sought guidance from a fitness professional, and made healthier food choices. Their consistent actions aligned with their intention led to a significant improvement in their overall well-being.

OVERCOMING FEAR AND SELF DOUBT

Fear and self-doubt are natural human emotions that arise when we face uncertainty or the possibility of failure. They often stem from past experiences, societal expectations, or the fear of judgment. Reflect on a situation in which fear or self-doubt prevented you from pursuing a goal or taking a risk.

For example, imagine you have a dream of starting your own business. However, fear of failure and self-doubt creep in, making you hesitate to take the necessary steps. As a result, you remain stuck in your comfort zone, feeling unfulfilled and longing for something more.

Take a moment to think about the fears and self-doubt that are currently holding you back. Write them down and acknowledge their presence. Recognize that these emotions are a normal part of the human experience, but they do not define your potential or limit your ability to make things happen.

To overcome fear and self-doubt, we must challenge the validity of our beliefs and develop strategies to move forward. Think about a time when you pushed past your fear and accomplished something significant. How did you find the courage to move forward despite the doubts and uncertainties? What were the rewards and lessons learned from facing your fears head-on?

Consider the story of a person who dreamt of pursuing a career in the arts but feared rejection and criticism. Despite the fear, they gathered their courage, took art classes, and started showcasing their work. Over time, they built confidence, received positive feedback, and even sold their artwork. By confronting fear and self-doubt, they unlocked their true potential and realized their passion.

Try to reflect on the strategies you can employ to challenge fear and self-doubt. Consider seeking support from mentors or like-minded individuals who can provide encouragement and guidance. Write down positive affirmations that counter your self-doubt and repeat them daily. Visualize yourself confidently moving past your fears and achieving your goals.

Action is a powerful antidote to fear and self-doubt. Taking small steps and building on each success can significantly boost our confidence. Reflect on a situation in which you overcame fear or self-doubt by taking action and the impact it had on your self-confidence.

For example, imagine you had a fear of public speaking. By gradually exposing yourself to small speaking engagements, such as presenting to a small group of friends, you built your confidence over time. Each successful experience helped diminish your fear and increased your belief in your abilities.

In the face of fear and self-doubt, it is crucial to practice self-compassion. Acknowledge that fear and self-doubt are normal emotions and that everyone experiences them to some extent. Treat yourself with kindness and understanding, just as you would a dear friend facing similar challenges.

When you be free, reflect on how you can cultivate self-compassion in your own life. Write down affirmations or mantras that remind you to be kind to yourself during moments of fear and self-doubt. Take time for self-care activities that nourish your mind, body, and spirit.

EMBRACING RESILIENCE AND PERSISTANCE

Life is not always smooth sailing, and setbacks and challenges are inevitable. Imagine a situation where you encountered a significant obstacle or faced repeated failures in pursuit of a goal. Reflect on how you responded to these challenges and the resilience you demonstrated in persevering.

For example, let's say you had a goal of running a marathon. During training, you faced injuries, setbacks, and moments of doubt. However, your resilience and persistence pushed you to keep going. You sought medical guidance, adjusted your training plan, and developed mental fortitude. Finally, you crossed the finish line, proud of your accomplishment and the lessons learned along the way.

Consider the stories of individuals who have achieved remarkable success despite facing numerous obstacles. What qualities and mindset do they embody? How can their stories inspire you to cultivate resilience and persistence in your own journey?

Think about the journey of an entrepreneur who faced multiple rejections before finding success. Despite setbacks, they remained determined, learned from each failure, and adapted their approach. Through persistence and a never-give-up attitude, they ultimately built a thriving business.

Between the paragraphs, think about a current challenge you are facing. How can you approach it with resilience and a determination to keep going? Consider the strategies you can adopt to overcome setbacks, learn from failures, and stay committed to making things happen.

TAKING INSPIRED ACTION

Having dreams and setting intentions is important, but they remain mere wishes unless backed by inspired action. Imagine a situation where you took bold, decisive action aligned with your desires and aspirations. How did it feel to move beyond contemplation and step into the realm of action?

For instance, envision a person who dreamed of writing a book. They set their intention to write every day and took the inspired action of creating a writing schedule, seeking feedback from mentors, and committing to their craft. As a result, they completed their manuscript and achieved their dream of becoming a published author.

Consider a goal or dream that has been on your mind for a while. Between the paragraphs, imagine the possibilities that would unfold if you took one small step towards making it happen. How can you infuse your actions with intention, passion, and purpose?

Reflect on the choices you make each day. Are they moving you closer to your desired outcomes or keeping you stagnant? What actions can you take, starting today, to propel yourself forward and create the life you envision?

As we conclude this chapter on making things happen, remember that the power to shape your life lies within you. Each choice, each intention, and each action is an opportunity to move closer to your dreams. By confronting fear, cultivating resilience, and taking inspired action, you can transform your aspirations into reality. Now is the time to embark on this journey of self-empowerment, to embrace the challenges, and to create the life you truly desire. Are you ready to take the first step?

you can get what you really desire

What do you really want from life? There are two options:

1. You don't know
2. You think you know but you're not sure

This is why many people are restless, moving from job to job, house to house, and country to country.

Take a step back. And look at the issue at hand.

What do you want? Because the reality is that life is long enough to get what you really want.

Now, that doesn't mean you can have everything you want. It simply means you can get what you REALLY want.

The problem is that most of us will never find out what we really want.

You can achieve more than you think man.

Let's say you want to have some of the most desirable things in life:

1. A high-paying job
2. Fame
3. A rich social life

4. A 7-digit bank account
5. A strong body
6. A Villa
7. A private island
8. A Rolls Royce Boat Tail

Are these things out of reach? I don't think so. As **Gary Keller** and **Jay Papasan**, authors of The One Thing, said:

> *"Success is sequential, not simultaneous."*

This means you can achieve a lot, just not at the same time. You achieve one thing after the other.

When you follow this strategy, you can accomplish way more in life than you think. Most people fail because they try to do too many things at the same time and they try to do it too fast.

As **Keith Cunningham**, the author of The Road Less Stupid, said:

> *"All choices require a trade-off and sacrifice. You can have almost anything you want . . . you just can't have everything you want."*

When you combine the two above quotes, you have the recipe for success in life.

Focus on one thing at a time.

Focus on the things you REALLY want.

As **J. Cole** says in his song Love Yourz:

> *"On the road to riches, listen, this is what you'll find. The good news is, you came a long way. The bad news is, you went the wrong way."*

No one wants to go the wrong way. It just happens because we don't take enough time to think about the topic of this article.

2-3 years back, I thought I wanted to achieve the following things in my life :

1. Travel the world
2. Be a multi-millionaire
3. Own a bunch of sneakers worth 2-3 lakhs INR
4. Live in a island or some other place as such
5. Go to movies every weekend
6. Have a wardrobe full of LVs, Gucci and AX attires and stuff

As the time went by—and the more I learned about myself—I dropped most of those silly dreams.

I started to get rid of those desires because I tried many things. I tried dreaming and chasing those stuffs. I didn't like them.

Yeah, what? You will be happy every day? Of course not. You will be the same person with the same challenges. The only difference is that the sun is shining. But you get used to that real quick.

Get clear on what you want and become unapologetic

Look, I think this is one of the hardest things in life. It's certainly one of the hardest emotional things I had to do.

At some point, we all have to admit to ourselves that there are A LOT of things in life we don't like.

But for some weird reason, whether that's social pressure or the pressure to prove ourselves to others, we do things that we don't actually want to do.

Here's another very common thing: Living in big cities.

I know so many people who believe you must live in a big city, otherwise, you don't matter. If you don't live in Mumabi, New Delhi, Bangalore, Paris, Dubai, Singapore, Hyderabad, and so forth—you're a loser.

Says who? The people who live in cities, living a hopeless life, complaining about the bad quality of life there?

"But we have theaters!" That you never go to, yes.

Now, if you're a lover of theater it's a different thing. And that's my point.

What do you REALLY want in life?

The magic word is trade-offs. You must decide what you like and what you don't like. If you know that on a deep level, you can get after what you like. And since life is long enough, you can get everything that you really want.

The truth is that we humans are not that complicated. Most of us only want a few things in life. Just decide what those few things are for you and make them happen.

Be completely unapologetic to yourself about what you want. Once you know, look at yourself in the mirror and say, "This is who I am. Get used to it. I ain't changing myself. That's it"

Wake up with focus and confidence every day

Life is long and short at the same time. It's long enough to accomplish a lot. It's too short if you waste your time.

No matter what you do, **DON'T WASTE YOUR TIME.**

It's much better to go in the wrong direction for a while than to stay where you are. **Movement**. That's the key.

As a result, you will know what you want and don't want.

Make some decisions, move to different places, learn new skills, make some art, or do something that gets you excited.

Something that makes you wake up every day and says, "Let's go."

And then just boom, go to get that.

drain a few hours

Being productive doesn't mean utilizing every waking minute to do productive things. That's why I don't like "hustle culture." I don't need to be busy every minute.

Sometimes, spending a day doing various things around the house, maybe taking walk or doing some reading, can actually be more useful. These moments help us examine our lives.

But high achievers and ambitious people often have a problem with doing nothing. They feel like they need to be productive every single minute. So they get busy with minor things.

For example, when highly productive people have spare time, it's not unusual to see them making minor improvements to their business. They optimize their websites, clean up their shops, do more research on their industry, and so forth.

It's great to have the desire to improve yourself and your career. But you also don't want to be too extreme with busywork.

In his commencement speech at the University of Southern California, the billionaire **Charlie Munger** said that the one quality he especially admired about his business partner, **Warren Buffett**, was Buffett's ability to be a lifelong learner.

" "If you take Warren Buffett and watched him with a time clock, I would say half of all the time he spends is sitting on his couch and reading.""

GOOD VS BAD

Doing something that helps us, in the long run, is actually not a waste of time when you think about it. So how do you "waste" your time wisely?

Avoid spending too much time on social media. We both know that's not good for you. It's also a good opportunity to switch from being a consumer to a creator. As a creator, you want to spend time making something. At the same time, you can also discover new insights and inspiration.

Some time ago, I was talking to a friend who asked me for some book recommendations. He said he wanted something to read, but had no specific topic in mind. Which is also why he didn't know what to search for.

I suggested he check out a local bookstore instead. And he can pick whatever got his interest. He ended up spending half a day in the bookstore, browsing various books.

And that's how he discovered his passion for trail running: When he read the book, The White Spider by **Heinrich Harrer**. (again i bet, most of y'all dont know him). The book inspired him to join mountain hiking groups on the weekends. And from there, he upgraded into doing trail marathons.

The next time you're low on energy, or you feel like you're on autopilot, or you're stuck on something, you can try to focus on bigger fundamentals in your life or career.

Instead of worrying about the next action or social media post, take the time to read a few good books. Your next idea or design inspiration just might come from that.

If you're working on a new diet, this could mean not worrying so much about that Saturday night you went out eating with friends. Instead, focus on the 20 other meals you'll be taking throughout the week. The impact of those other meals is much more significant.

KILLING TIME WITH INTENTION

When it comes to achieving things, people often think about action. But as Buffett said,

"it's also about waiting for the right pitch. "

The mathematical statistician **Nassim Taleb**, author of Fooled by Randomness, a book about the randomness of success and failure, once observed:

"The only measure of success is how much time you have to kill."

Successful individuals understand that personal energy is limited. So it's important that we only spend our energy and time on things that matter most.

So what does this mean in daily life? It's all about being aware that it's okay to kill time. I call this: Killing time with intention.

That's because if you waste time deliberately, then it's not a waste. You did it with good intent. And the intent is to enjoy your life.

To be productive in the long term(directly or indirectly). And not to kill yourself by overworking for a few years and then burning out for an even longer time.

So, what are you doing this evening? Nothing?

stop comparing

When we think about success, we almost always make comparisons. That's how people end up chasing titles, recognition, number of followers, or more income. That's a shame because most people start with the best intentions. You might want to:

- Organize retreats
- Do more freelancing work for a a group of people who appreciate you
- Start a business by doing work you enjoy, and that creates value
- Invest in companies that are undervalued as of now

So you start out well. You do the right thing. You educate yourself. You get after it.

But after working a while, you get bored. Results might not come as quickly as you expected. The work is hard. People are ignoring you.

During those times, you need to be better. But instead, you get distracted by comparing yourself to others. That's destructive behavior. Comparing oneself to others has destroyed many people's good intentions. Life is about accepting that everyone's situation is unique. We're all on our own trajectory. Our careers, families, relationships, mental and emotional health, and so forth are different from others. Other factors like talent, stress-tolerance, financial and social resources, educational background, and so forth also come into play.

Too many people forget about those things. So when things don't work out, they get discouraged and depressed. Lack of success doesn't make you a failure.

Not succeeding in a paticular job or field of study doesn't make you a failure. It's also meaningless if you're successful at making money but are miserable because you sacrificed all other aspects of life.(whether its social or personal,whatever)

We define what true success means for us. We don't even have to measure it at all. Some people go through life without having any career goals or income goals. If that works, why not?

I love to set goals that are within my control. That helps me to stay motivated and to keep moving forward. The key is to figure out how you work best.

COMPARE YOURSELF WITH YOUR PAST SELF

Look, I'm not a fan of comparing yourself to others, no matter what. I just don't see any benefit in that.

Sure, it's great to not have an ego and be open to learning from others. But you don't have to compare yourself when you learn from others.

As a student, I look up to my seniors and who have passed out from my dream college, and I've learned a lot from studying his advice and actions. But I will never look at my results and compare them to his. Why?

If you want to measure your progress, it's best to look at yourself. This is one of the most important lessons that **Jordan Peterson** shares in his book, 12 Rules For Life. He said:

> ""*Don't compare yourself with other people; compare yourself with who you were yesterday.*""

I look at my academic results and achievements in the past and compare them to my current. For example, when i was studying for medical exams, i could not do well. In the past, I would worry. Now, I don't. I simply stick to my current stream (i shifted to comm) and realize that mistakes recover in time.

I just keep improving myself. If you're reading this, it means you care about personal growth. It also means you're closer to success than other people who don't even bother to think about it.

Just remind yourself of that. As long as you're learning and improving, you're on the right path. There's no need to be concerned with what others do. *Who cares, anyway?*

skip some of the tasks to make life easier

Sometimes you run into a challenge that stops you in your tracks. And you have this voice in your head that says, "**I NEED to solve this thing. Otherwise, I can't move on to next.**"

Just like when you take tests in school, and you would run into a question you didn't have the answer to?

What do you do when you run into a challenge like that? Do you keep trying hard to remember the answer or to solve the problem?

Or do you skip the question and finish the test first before you come back to it? For many years, I did the former. I always assumed you needed to complete a test from start to finish.

I used to be pretty anxious before taking tests till my Class 10th. But then, a teacher told me, "Just skip a question you don't have the answer to." This advice was golden to me as a kid.

Previously, I thought things like, "What if I get stuck?"

Now, I think, "So what if I get stuck? I'll just skip it!"

WHY MOMENTUM MATTERS

If you want to accomplish anything in life, whether it's acing a test, writing a book, or starting a business, momentum is everything.

We all know how good it feels to get excited about something new. Maybe you want to form a daily walking habit, or maybe you want to start working out every morning, or watering the plants.

You get started, and after a few weeks, you get stuck. You want to go for a walk, but you run into your friends in the market.

What most people do is this: They give up on their goal. It takes something really small to stop your momentum. You just have to get emotional for a day. And then, you get inside your own head.

It's just like taking that test in school. When your test has 20 questions and you only have 60 minutes to complete it, you don't want to stop for 30 minutes at question 3.

You won't only waste time when you stop for too long. What's worse, you also waste energy when you struggle.

YOU TRY TO MAKE THINGS ZERO-EFFORTED

Sometimes you just have to be strategic about skipping things. Especially if you want to make progress in life. Both our time and energy are limited, and it's easy to lose sight of what really matters.

For example, if you want to build a career, you sometimes need to skip watching series every night or cooking delicious meals every single night.

Last year, I had the idea to write a book about some average indian coolege scenario. I started the book, but I soon got stuck. I just didn't enjoy writing it at the time, so I got rid of it. I moved on to gaming instead but why? because, for me it took zero efforts while gaming.

You want to skip some things because you don't want to expend more energy on things than necessary. Life and work are already hard. Why make it harder for yourself by being so rigid?

You want to be flexible and get used to what comes your way(*dynamic,we can say*)**. And sometimes, the best way to make progress is to decide NOT to do something.**

how does it feel to be wise

What does it mean to be wise? To me, it has nothing to do with a person's IQ or degree. A wise person is someone who applies common sense. That sounds paradoxical, right? Common sense is common after all. It's about the insights, lessons, and wisdom everyone knows. But the problem is that not everyone applies what they know.

In fact, it's very uncommon to see people applying common sense. I know a few people who I consider as wise, and none of them are considered geniuses. They're just reliable, experienced, calm, and good people who live normal lives.

Mentioning down, what I saw in wise people:

RELY ON FACTS RATHER THAN ASSUMING

Most people make assumptions without realizing it. Every time we're not sure about something, we're making assumptions. If I send someone an email about a collab proposal, and they don't get back to me in two days, and I think they're not interested, I'm making an assumption.

The belief that someone is not interested because they don't instantly respond is just an idea that's not based on facts.

As long as I don't get a response in that scenario, I can't say whether we have a deal or not. In our daily lives, we make countless of these assumptions. And most of our judgments are based on our personal beliefs. The problem is we can't trust our beliefs simply because they are so subjective.

Instead, rely on facts and avoid interpreting everything based on your ideas, beliefs, and feelings. A quick shortcut you can apply is this: Observe your thoughts and ask yourself, "How do I know what I'm thinking is true?" You often find that you either need to ask more questions, do research, or simply wait until you receive feedback.

THINK FROM FIRST PRINCIPLES

Thinking from first principles was coined by the Ancient Greek philosopher, **Aristotle**. **Elon Musk** explained this idea really succinctly in an interview with Kevin Rose.

Some people assume that thinking from first principles means you don't make assumptions. But for Musk, it means you go even beyond looking at facts.

In the interview he gave an example of how people looked at the cost of batteries:

> ""*People would say, 'Historically it cost $600 per kilowatt-hour, and so it's not going to be much better than that in the future.' And you say, No, what are the batteries made of? First-principles means you say: Okay, what are the material constituents of the batteries?*""

Sometimes the facts of today will limit you. At some point, the cost of batteries was at a certain level, but that doesn't mean the cost cannot decrease. Thinking from first principles is a way to challenge the status quotient. It's looking at what is, and thinking what could be, keeping the laws of human nature and physics in mind.

Wise people constantly ask, **"Is there a better way we can do this?"**

READ!!!

Every wise person I know has a very broad set of knowledge, ranging from history to economics to politics to blah blah everythingg. We're all equipped with this fascinating brain that's the perfect substance for solving problems.

But that instrument needs energy and food to properly function. Feeding your body is easy: *You eat.*

But what about feeding your mind? This is something not a lot of people take seriously. Most people's days consist of work and leisure. At what moment do you nurture your mind?

It's when you're intellectually challenged. That doesn't happen a lot at our work or social interactions. And it sure as hell doesn't happen when we're consuming entertaining content.

The best way to challenge yourself on an intellectual level is to acquire knowledge. The easiest way to do that is to read a book. You can also listen to a book or take a course. Wise people do something that challenges their minds every day. They read a lot. And they read widely because most mental stimuli comes from learning about new things.

TAKE TIME TO MAKE DECISIONS

In our fast-paced world, many people think that smart people are "quick on their feet." But making good decisions is not always a product of quickness. In some situations, it pays off to be a quick decision-maker.

But we often become quick decision-makers by first becoming slow decision-makers. This sounds contary, but it's the same process as running a marathon. No one runs a marathon on their first run. Similarly, no good decision-maker can be quick at the beginning of their career.

It's important to take as much time as you can to decide. But no more. Otherwise we risk procrastinating for no good reason.

LISTEN TO OTHERS WILL ALL EARS

I find it funny that the most ignorant people have difficulty listening to advice while the smartest people are usually the first to listen to everyone. I remember when one of my social science teachers asked me about my opinion about the 2008 financial crisis when I was in class 9.

"Where do we go from here?" He asked me. What did I know as a secondary student back then? And yet, my teacher took the time to listen to what I had to say. And he was really curious as well.

Ever since that moment, I've been extremely aware of how often I'm curious about other people's opinions and insight. My experience is that almost no one cares. Most people just love to listen to their own voice and don't care about what others have to say.

The wise people I know are the opposite. They love to learn from others and are always open to different ideas.

LEARN FROM MISTAKES

Wise people see mistakes as lessons. **Ralph Waldo Emerson** said it best:

> "*"Good judgment comes from experience, and a lot of that comes from bad judgment.*" "

We all make bad judgments and mistakes. That's not what matters. How do you respond after you make a mistake? That's the key.

Do you use it to learn? Or do you become more risk-bearing after every mistake you make? The former will help you grow, the latter will advance your destruction.

As you go through life, it's important to realize it's okay to make mistakes. The smartest people in the world don't necessarily make fewer mistakes. They just don't let their mistakes go to waste.

There's one overarching theme to all the things I've learned from wise people: **They make sure they get something positive and useful out of every interaction.** Everything they do feeds on top of everything else they do.

That's how you create a **positive cycle** for yourself. That means your life will only get better.

being successful and happy are different

What are some features that make you successful a? Let's go over a few things that a lot of people who're doing well usually do:

1. **Sacrifice the present for tomorrow**: People who achieve substantial goals usually spend years getting there. An athlete who wins a gold medal at the Olympics usually dedicates their whole life to the end goal of winning.

2. **Working through pain**: We're all human beings, and human beings get hurt, physically and mentally. People who succeed usually succeed despite being hurt. They have a higher pain tolerance. They persevere.

3. **Single-minded focus**: When someone has a very high aim, they give that aim almost all their attention and energy. They just do that one thing for years.

Depending on the type of person you ask, you'll get a different response based on the above. Some people say, "That's the only way to succeed." And other people say, "That's just too much."

Whether you like it or not, the only way to achieve things that most people don't is to do what most people never do. And some of those things are listed above. But those things will not lead to happiness. We need different traits to become happy.

Success and happiness are two different things

A lot of people assume that success leads to happiness. "If I achieve this particular goal, I will be happy." That type of conditional thinking only leads to unhappiness.

Happiness is a state of mind that only happens in the present moment. And your state of mind can be different from moment to moment. The ultimate goal of meditation is to reach a state of mind that's consistently tranquil—free from suffering.

But success is not a state of mind. It's a process with a beginning and an end. You set a goal, you start working on it, and you either succeed or fail. Either way, there's a moment of reckoning.

Happiness doesn't have that moment. And if it does, the moment is brief. I remember when I finished secondary school. Throughout the years I studied till 10th, I kept thinking, "Oh man, I can't wait till I finish 10th. I will feel so much better."

You can guess what happened. I passed, felt great for a few days, and then went back to my default state—which was mostly restless at the time because I prioritize success over happiness.

What's your default state of mind?

Let me ask you a few questions so we can figure out what your default state of mind is.

- Are you working towards a big goal in your life right now? Think of getting a gold medal, starting a new task, switching careers, aiming for 100 percent, etc.
- Do you feel like today is a means towards your goal?
- Are you looking forward to the day you achieve your goal?
- Do you assume your life will be any different after that point?

If you answered yes more than twice, you're like most of us who are overly focused on the future. Your default state of mind is, "I want to succeed."

It's not bad. Your focus on a specific goal will help you to improve your life. The opposite is to do nothing and waste your life. I never like it when people want to make you feel bad for being ambitious. The people who continuously preach that you should take it easy and not set goals should keep that to their own community of unambitious folks.

I love to set goals and work on improving my life and career. It's what drives human improvement. But I also want to be happy along the way. Those two things are not mutually always exclusive. It requires a different focus.

Prioritizing happiness today

Look, you know what it takes to feel happy today. Just look at the source of your unhappiness, and get it out of your life. What causes unhappiness? Here's how I rank the causes:

1. Overthinking: The biggest cause of unhappiness is our own minds. If we can stop listening to our thoughts and focus on what's in front of us, we instantly feel better.

2. Being in bad shape: When you don't work out and eat a lot of junk food, you feel bad physically. And when your body feels bad by your own doing, you also feel bad mentally. Being sick or injured is different because you can't control that. But being in bad shape is something you do to yourself.

3. Dead-end career: You spend most of your time at work, and if you despise your job, it's no wonder you don't feel happy. I'm not the type who says you should just accept it. No, you can invest in yourself, learn new skills, and find another job or career.

4. Negative friends: Some people are annoying and negative. Being around those people is not good for your state of mind. You'd rather be rid of them than have them in your life.

As you can see it's not easy. We have to make some difficult choices to be happy.

But all these choices happen in the present. And you can't solve it by just tolerating pain. Sure, that works for achieving your goals. But not for happiness.

If you simply take care of at least two of the things on the list above, you will instantly feel better. And the good news is that all these things are within your control. Which one will you work on first?

Resources

1. Various websites and articles for statistical info
2. Numerous websites for exact quotes and personalities
3. Self-help guides and books for reference
4. Articles by one of my fav author (*can't name*)
5. friends and teachers for ideas and povs
6. newspapers and blogs for reference